The Complete Book of Hugs

The Complete Book of Hugs

Ricky Friedel

Illustrations by Laurie LaFrance

M. Evans and Company, Inc.

New York

M. Evans and Company, Inc.

216 East 49th Street

New York, New York 10017

Library of Congress Cataloging-in-Publication Data

Friedel, Ricky.
    The complete books of hugs / Ricky Friedel.
        p. cm.
    ISBN 0-87121-827-X
    1. Hugging I. Title.
BF637.H83F75 1998
158.2—dc21   97-45981

Book design by Wendy Bass

Manufactured in the United States of America

First Edition

9 8 7 6 5 4 3 2 1

to Jill

—INTRODUCTION

The need is as old as time itself. As old as man, and woman, and you. It's a yearning that starts in the cradle and goes on forever, the world's greatest source of comfort and pleasure, that thing we call a hug. Hugging, quite simply is magic in motion. It's the perfect solution to most of life's problems. There is nothing else like it; nothing even comes close. And it is something you need right now.

When you were small, and hugs felt so large, your life was a never-ending hug. The right hug at the right time made the world a warm, fuzzy place, and sometimes it made it a miraculous place. When you had that hug you had it all. Life was good. Life was great. Life was one big smile. But somehow growing up meant giving all that up...or at least that's what we thought. What on earth were we thinking?

Everyone needs lots of hugs! Big ones, small ones, long ones and short ones; fat ones, skinny ones, tame ones and wild ones. Squeezes, squishes, rubdowns and takedowns; thrillers, chillers, grabbers and gropers. By moonlight, by starlight, by candlelight or by flashlight. Even in the broadest of daylight...there's no such thing as too many hugs.

Hugs are the stuff that dreams are made of—our greatest natural resource. They cost us nothing, but give us everything. And they don't require a degree. They're food for the body, for the mind, and for the soul. And they don't contain a single calorie. So what are you waiting for? What's holding you back? You need to get out there and hug!!!

This book is your passport to the incredible world of truly amazing hugs. Hugging may be a lost art, but this book is going to help you find it. There is much to learn (over one hundred different hugs, the last time we counted), but it requires nothing more than your desire and your enthusiasm. It doesn't matter if you're five or ninety-five. It doesn't matter if you're a total novice who doesn't even like to shake hands or a practiced professional with "hugs of steel." It doesn't matter if you're in love, in lust, in longing, or in Los Angeles (see special earthquake hugs). This book is absolutely guaranteed to open your arms, melt your heart, expand your horizons, and increase your huggability…instantaneously!

But a word of warning to those about to begin hugging: Once you get started, there's probably no turning back. Hugs can be all-consuming, highly contagious, and, in some cases, totally addictive. Hugs can become your fountain of youth. Hugs can become your very best friend. Hugs can become your reason for living. How lucky can you get!

The Basic Hug

Recommended Usage: When you're feeling a little rusty, out of practice, self-conscious, or totally terrified; or when you can't even remember the last time you had a hug.

In hugging, as in life, the right attitude is far more important than perfect technique, especially if you're just getting started. So the very first thing you need to do is send your inner critic out for a walk, and lock the door behind it.

Stand facing your partner, with about three feet between you, and open your arms wide. Approach slowly, sliding your arms around each other just below shoulder height. Now squeeze, just firmly enough to impart your message of love, friendship, reassurance, or just plain goodwill. When you are feeling content (remembering that in this first hug, moderation can be a virtue) prepare to disengage. Now gently let go.

Note: A slow, caring "release" is an integral part of every hug; swift or abrupt departures should be avoided wherever possible.

The "I Love You" Hug (a.k.a., The Heartstopper)

Recommended Usage: When cupid's arrow has hit its mark.

When you're lucky enough to feel real love, you need to let that person know. Don't assume they know because you said it yesterday. And don't assume they know because you said "I love you" an hour ago. You need to say it over and over, from the crack of dawn till the time you say goodnight. And you need to make it as clear as you can by supporting your words with a very special hug.

This is the hug that says you're the greatest. It says you're together, and that you'll never be apart. It's the hug that promises forever and ever. The hug that hands over your heart.

When you have found love, you have found it all. Life will never be the same. And isn't that the way you want it? So don't be embarrassed by the strength of your feelings. Let that strength come through in your loving hug. You can never be too rich, too thin, or too hugged. Especially if you're being hugged by the one you love.

The Once in a Lifetime Hug

Recommended Usage: When the planets align, the stars align, and you have a perfect moment with someone you love.

The planets are in synch, your biorhythms are up, and you're looking straight into the eyes of the one you love. Maybe you're at the top of the Eiffel Tower. Maybe you're at the bottom of the Great Barrier Reef. Or maybe you're just coming home from work. But in that moment, nothing else matters but the powerful feelings you can't contain. All that's missing is a 90-piece orchestra, and Steven Spielberg's special effects. So make your own music, and light your own fireworks, by capturing this moment with an unforgettable hug.

Whether you're low in the valley or high in the mountains, it's one of life's peak experiences. It is the hug by which all others will be measured. A magic moment to be cherished and savored. It could only have happened with the perfect person, but if you stay with that person it will happen again.

The Good Morning Hug
(a.k.a., The Good to the Last Drop Hug)

Recommended Usage: When the best part of waking up ain't Folger's in your cup.

Some people get up each morning because the alarm clock tells them they have to. Their get-up-and-go got up and went a very long time ago, and the best part of waking up truly is the Folger's in their cup.

But you don't need any java. You've got something else to get you going in the morning. Something else to start your engine to squeeze the daylights into you. So while the rest of the world wakes up moaning and groaning, you wake up rejoicing because you can open your eyes each morning and see the one you love. And when you take each other in your arms, it's more than enough incentive to get to work, if not to conquer the world.

There is so very little in life that can compare to your precious morning hug. So don't ever try to bolt out of bed and miss your reason for living. If every day could begin with a hug, you wouldn't really care how it ended.

The "Not Tonight, I Have a Headache" Hug (a.k.a., The Anticlimax)

Recommended Usage: When sleep is the only thing on your mind, and you don't want to know what's on his.

This hug will stop him in his tracks. It is your way of saying I love you to death, but DON'T EVEN THINK ABOUT GETTING ANY! Start with a kind and gentle embrace, so he knows it's not really his fault. But the moment his hands start to make their move, grab them tight to cut off his options. Now push him back, spin him around, and send him out to get you some aspirin.

Consider it a cold front that blew in from the west. Or a mood that just blew in from the past. Or hormones that just came up from the equator. Consider it whatever makes you feel best, but consider the matter closed for discussion. Tonight your electric blanket is your best and only friend. And if he were smart, he'd plug his in too.

The "I Hate My Job" Hug

Recommended Usage: When you're killing yourself for the company line, and you've yet to hear a single thank you.

Your office is tiny. Your paycheck is smaller. And your boss is a total jerk. Every Monday you wish it were Friday, and every Friday you wish you could quit. It's a way of life for millions of people. But how did it happen to you?

You need to vent. You need to cry. You need to scream, "I hate my job!!!!!" But what you need most is to be held in the arms of the one you love, and reassured that this horrendous job, and the lack of lifestyle it affords you is all just temporary. So take a slightly longer lunch and rendezvous with the one who counts. Have your cry in some supportive arms. Tell him of your woes. And be thankful for everything wonderful you do have in your life, because love is more important than work.

This afternoon you'll go back to the office, and if you don't feel any better, start working on your resume and your resignation letter. Life is just too precious to miss because of your job.

The "Make the World Go Away" Hug
(a.k.a., The "I Want My Mommy" Hug)

Recommended Usage: When the only thing that's standing between you and the big, bad world is a consoling pair of arms.

You're an adult now—at least that's what it says on your driver's license. And everyone is coming to you for the answers. Your secretary…Your boss…Your mother…Even your precocious six-year-old daughter. Well, right now you don't feel very adult, you feel about six-years-old too, and you wish there was someone you could turn to for all those answers.

Well, there is someone. And while this person may not have *all* the answers, this person does have a magic potion that can make you feel all better for a very long time. Who is this special person? Actually, it's anyone who loves you…your best friend, your mom, even your six-year-old daughter. If they can give you a warm, loving hug, they're giving you what you need most right now.

Being an adult is a really tough job, and you need a vacation that starts today. So let down your adult walls. And hold your adult calls. It's time to play seek and hide. Seek those arms, and hide in their shelter: that's how this game is played. Even if a hug can't make the world go away, it can keep it at a safer distance. Within just minutes it certainly feels lighter because it isn't all resting on your shoulders. And sooner than you would have ever imagined, you can look it squarely in the eye.

9

The Looking for "Mr. Right" Hug

Recommended Usage: When you need to know this very minute if the magic may last a lifetime.

After kissing so many dozens of frogs, and watching them all turn into snakes and dogs and chickens and weasels, you almost gave up hope. Until today. Until him.

Could this be the man you have been waiting a lifetime to find? Could he truly be "Mr. Right"? Yes, he makes you feel different than you've ever felt before. More safe. More secure. More yourself. But can you trust this feeling? The way he holds you may hold the answer.

So let him hold you now. Do you feel his heart open as his arms open? Do you feel completely cherished by his embrace? Do you feel complete and content? Then your search may be over. These may be the arms you will want around you forever. Because dreams do come true for those who have never stopped dreaming.

The Perfect Fit Hug

Recommended Usage: When you're looking for a sign that he's really the one you were meant to spend your life with.

Like two pieces in a puzzle, you're the perfect fit—two different bodies that were made to connect. And every time you hug that puzzle feels solved. He may be tall, while you're fairly small; he may be bulky, while you're very slim. But nothing has ever felt this good, or looked this good, or been this good.It's God's way of telling you that the search is truly over.

So whenever you lose sight of why you're still together, take some time out to put those pieces back in place.

Reexperience the magic of "the perfect fit," two bodies destined to always be joined.The hugs start here, and this is where they stay. Like the commercial says, nothing else comes close.

The Truly, Madly, Deeply Hugged Hug

Recommended Usage: When there aren't enough words (or adverbs) in the world to express how completely loved you feel.

It's true. You're mad about him. And you're in so deep you may never get out. You are drowning in a sea of his affections. You can no longer see the shore. What could be more glorious! What could be more profound!

So don't fight it. Surrender your heart to this captain of the high seas and surrender yourself to his willing arms. Feel his tenderness. Feel his touch. Feel the power of his intent. Feel the promise in his strength. And feel yourself floating in his embrace.

This man loves you and wants you. His hug makes that clear. Let him sail you off into the sunset to begin a life together. You are truly, madly, deeply hugged, truly madly deeply loved, and the envy of all who see.

The "I Hope He Doesn't Try to Kiss Me" Hug

Recommended Usage: When you want to be sure that the blind date from hell knows exactly where you stand.

The blind date of your dreams has turned into a nightmare, and you can't wait to get home and forget it ever happened. So why doesn't he feel the same way? You know that you want out, but he looks like he wants in, and the goodbye battle is about to begin.

You're certain he's ready to storm the Bastille. He's starting to pucker up. And you can tell that he wants to scale your ramparts and devour your precious jewels. So pull up the drawbridge and summon the guards. And use a hug to head him off at the pass—a hug that's as cold as a sword forged from steel. Your lips are reserved for men in shining armor, but this guy hasn't even been to "knight school." His sexual chemistry flunked biology. He needs to saddle up and go home.

In less than a second the hug is over, and he knows that it's over for him. So see you later, alligator; go play with your friends in the moat. In the future, you'll stay home with a really good book, or watch "Robin Hood" reruns on your VCR. You swear it on your Maidenform, and on your lovely maiden form: you don't care how bad things get, this is your last blind date.

The First Date Hug

Recommended Usage: When a kiss might be too much, but anything less might be too little.

It was a perfect first date (the first you can remember). He took you to your favorite restaurant, but that was just the beginning. The candles glowed and the conversation never lagged. You laughed together. You talked forever. He seemed genuinely interested in everything you had to say. And to top it off, he's really cute!

You wish the evening would never end but you know that it needs to end soon. Though your mind and body are racing with future hopes and dreams, you need to hold your ground. If something is worth having, it's worth waiting for (you've made that mistake before). And this is definitely worth having. So what do you do now?

A handshake would be too cold, and your kiss would be too hot, but a hug was made for moments like this—a hug that's filled with hope. Not too tight and not too long. Nothing out of control. But enough to say you really care, to say you've just begun.

Now say goodnight and close the door and sigh a long deep sigh. The future is open for love and romance, and that's enough to make you high.

The Last Date Hug
(a.k.a., The Dishonorable Discharge)

Recommended Usage: When you realize that life is too short to spend another minute with him.

He may be rich and handsome, he may be smooth and sweet-talking, he may be everything you thought you wanted in a man. But now you know he's not for you, and it's time to move on. Not every relationship is meant to be; and some men are very long on potential but all too short on follow through.

So when he closes in to claim his prize, you need to let him know you're no longer available. You don't need to push him away, you just need to tell him that the party's over and it's time to say goodbye. This is the hug that says, "we're just friends—friends that are about to become strangers." It says, "I can't wait to get out of here and to leave you far behind." Give it no energy, give it no life, and you're giving him the message he's got coming. Then go home and celebrate with a glass of Champagne. You've survived another round in the arena called romance, and you're a stronger person for making it through.

The Morning Glory Hug

Recommended usage: When life is getting tough, and mornings are getting even tougher.

You think to yourself, "God, why should I get out of bed?" If the heavens suddenly part and you get an answer, leap from the bed and hide under some heavy furniture. But if not, your only salvation is to gaze across the pillow into the eyes of your beloved. (Note: If you do not recognize the person gazing back at you, move immediately to the "Do I know you?" Hug.)

Drink in the nectar of your partner's loving gaze. Then, as you feel your rapture about to overflow, slowly wrap your arms around your partner and join every body part that nature will allow (and nature allows a lot!). This is one of the few hugs where lip service may be included at no extra charge, so be sure to press your mouths into active duty, morning breath be damned!

WARNING: Once you start this hug it may be necessary to cancel all of your morning appointments. In extreme cases, you may have to cancel an entire month's appointments. When life starts to feel this good, why *should* you get out of bed?

The "You're Snoring" Hug
(a.k.a., The Silencer)

Recommended Usage: Between the hours of 1 A.M. and 6 A.M. when the only thing you want in life is a good night's sleep.

You absolutely adore the beautiful human being sleeping soundly beside you. But if the snoring doesn't stop, you may have to strangle him. What do you do when your life is turning into a sleep deprivation experiment? How do you salvage the relationship without resigning yourself to separate bedrooms? Enter the "You're Snoring" Hug.

This hug is like a great cup of coffee. It starts off warm and soothing, as you gently rub his arm, his back, or his tummy. And just like that cup of coffee, it ends with a jolt, as you give one good body shove to completely startle your sweetie. Then it's back to sleep you go. Immediately. By the time he opens his eyes to see what hit him, yours are closed tight. Instead of seeing a hostile presence beside him, all he sees is his angelic partner, fast asleep and lost in dreams. At least that's what he thinks he's seeing. Confused, but too exhausted to figure it out, he'll conclude it was all just a bad dream, and drift back off to slumber. By morning, it's forgotten. By him, anyway. And that's what counts·

The "Marry Me!" Hug

Recommended Usage: When you know it's time to tie the knot, and your arms are the string that will do the tying.

Your search is over—you have found your future, a woman you would be proud to have as your bride. It's time to let her know, to say it with words that are so crystal clear that the message is surely delivered. Let your hug be the special messenger.

Hold her in your arms and look deep in her eyes. Don't let anything break your gaze. Now say loud and clear, "Marry me. Marry me!" And prepare to become the luckiest man in the world. When two lives become one, time stands still. Tied in a love knot, your hearts beating fast, this moment will always be remembered. Friends will ask you to tell the story and your children will ask you to tell the story. It's the story that no one will ever tire of, as long as love exists.

The Pull-the-Plug Hug
(a.k.a., The Last Squeeze)

Recommended Usage: When your relationship has run out of juice, and it's time to take him off your life support system.

He promises the moon. He promises the stars. Promises, promises, promises. But all you get is grief. (See also "Liar, Liar, Pants on Fire" Hug)

This relationship has been over forever. So why can't you get it to end? Because you love him. Well…you used to love him. Well…you thought you loved him. What were you thinking?

It's time to pull the plug on this lifeless connection. It's time to pull the plug once and for all, so you can get on with your life and find the love you deserve. So the next time he comes within hugging distance, seize him with enthusiasm and usher him toward the door. Turn the knob and open it wide, all the while maintaining your strong stride. Then with one last little push the deed will be fully done. Out into the cold he goes and out of your life for keeps. You've taken out the trash and now you're free at last.

The Honeymoon Hug

Recommended Usage: When you've both said "I do," and now it's time to do it.

Shake all that rice out of your hair and say goodbye to your nearest and dearest. Toss the bouquet to some lucky single. Then get into the limo and get out of town, to a place real private where you're all alone.

As you cross over the threshold, hugging in each other's arms, you know that your wedding was not a dream. You did it.

Tomorrow morning it will be breakfast in bed. Then lunch in bed. Then dinner in bed. And that's your schedule for the rest of the week. And in between all this dining and "dancing," try to catch a few winks of sleep. Everyone always remembers their honeymoon, that special moment when time stood still. And every time you hug from now on, you'll remember that threshold, you'll remember that hug, and you'll remember the reasons you said "I do."

The Love Handle Hug
(a.k.a., The Something to Hang On to Hug)

Recommended Usage: When every day you have a little more to love, and that's the way you like it.

Some women like their guys taut and lean—guys who look like Chippendale dancers. But you prefer the comfort of a Chippendale chair, and you like your guy with extra meat on his bones. Those extra pounds are soft to snuggle and they give you a cushion to break life's little falls.

So let him know now how much you love him, and how much you love his excess baggage by grabbing that baggage by the two love handles and giving him a gentle squeeze. He may be slightly overweight, but he's not over the limit. And he doesn't need to spend half his life in the gym. He cares more about you than he cares about his appearance, and guys like that can be rare.

The Too Big to Handle Hug
(a.k.a., The "You're a Quart Low on Your Slimfast" Hug)

Recommended Usage: When every day you have a little more to love, but you'd be happier with a little less (see also The "What a Waist!" Hug).

Some people say that bigger is better, but you say that bigger can be a little too big. What happened to that gorgeous body you fell in love with—the one you could stare at for hours and hours. You used to be able to wrap your arms around his waist; now your two hands don't even touch. You know too much of a good thing when you feel it, and this is way way way too much. It's kind of cute, but it's also kind of scary, and sometimes enough is enough.

So use this hug to show him with love that it's time he started to downsize. Grab his love handles and hold on tight; tell him you won't let go until they're gone. If not for the sake of his heart and his health, then for the sake of his wardrobe that no longer fits. He has passed the point of pleasantly plump and you're concerned that he doesn't ever want to go back. But he needs to go back before he no longer can, and you've just delivered this message by hand.

The Hug Lite (half the fat, twice the fun)

Recommended Usage: When the scales have just tipped in your direction and you're ready to celebrate with some sinfully rich affection.

Those bun-burning workouts have been paying off and you can practically see the pounds slip away. But now it's time for a special treat—the one you call your sweetie. We're not talking candy or cookies or cake. We're not talking ice cream or mousse or pie. We're talking about the person you're doing this for, the one special love that you adore.

So jump into your partner's arms without any fear that he can carry the weight. Grab on tonight to this hot fudge sundae and gobble him up like the best dessert. Is there anything in the world that could taste any better? Is there anything that leaves your tummy so full?

When you like your body it's so fun to share it, especially with someone who wants you this much. And the slimmer you are, the closer he can get, proving that food is no substitute for a menu of love.

The One-a-Day Hug

Recommended Usage: Take one every morning before breakfast. Repeat every hour if necessary.

Once in the morning is usually enough, though twice or three times is always better. It doesn't have to last long to last you through the day, and it relieves your sense of longing. Some people take Centrum and some people take Flintstones, but you need to take someone in your arms every morning.

It's better to skip a meal or two than it is to skip your daily hug. Because a hug a day keeps the doctor away, unless the doctor is doing the hugging. So make the time even if you don't have the time. Wake up early if that's what you must do. A few extra minutes first thing in the morning will make all the difference in the rest of your day. Studies have proved it and experts agree: nothing is more nutritious than a daily hug.

The Honeymoon Is Over Hug
(a.k.a., The Stranger in My Bed Hug)

Recommended Usage: When fantasies fade, and reality strikes with a vengeance.

He perspires. She snores. He scratches. She burps. He likes Chinese food. She likes Italian food. He wants to eat with chopsticks. She wants to eat in bed.

In the beginning, love is pure magic. But when the honeymoon is over, it's a struggle to keep finding the silver lining in all those clouds. It's out of the bliss and into the blisters because the only thing that's going to get you through is a lot of hard work.

You need to start that hard work with a heartwarming hug, a hug that says you truly believe the best is yet to come. There is no such thing as the perfect partner, except for the ones that we see on TV. Being in a relationship means being human, and allowing others to be the same.

The "Is Anybody Out There?" Hug

Recommended Usage: When you've been taking on the world by yourself too long, and you need to feel some company.

You're independent, self-reliant, and resourceful; you have money and freedom and friends. You've made it thus far almost all on your own, but you're beginning to wonder if this is all there is. Lately, you've been asking yourself, "Where's the beef?" Or, more precisely, "Where's the beefcake?"

So why not postpone that important meeting and start putting first things first. You've been busy before and kept a lot of guys waiting, but it's time to let at least one guy in. Maybe it's the guy you turned down last weekend, or that cute new guy who delivers your mail; maybe it's the guy who lives up the street, or your doctor, your lawyer, or your indian chief. All these guys are ripe with potential, but you're the one who has to start picking the fruit. Then like a runner who just finished a marathon, which is often the way you feel, collapse into this new prospect's arms and let him revive you with his powerful hug. He may not be perfect and he may not be permanent, but if he knows how to hug, you he'll do for now.

The "Honey, I'm Home!" Hug

Recommended Usage: When you've given all day at the office, and you're ready to receive.

Day after day it's the same old drill and you're really starting to tire. It's early to rise, early to bed, and nothing but work in between. There has to be more to life right now than being a good soldier. And every night you discover that "more" the moment you come home and open the front door.

It may be a jungle "out there" where you work, but her housewarming embrace can turn a lion into a pussycat. And despite a day that's as tough as yours, she still has the strength to make you purr. So open the door, put down your briefcase, and cry out, "Hi Honey, I'm home!" Then reap the rewards of all your hard work as she showers you with affection that's fit for a king. A man's home may be his castle, but it would be nothing without his queen.

The "I Want a Baby" Hug

Recommended Usage: When your biological clock is ticking loud, and the alarm is about to ring.

It's not a craze. It's not a fad. It's parenthood, and you want in. You want a baby and you want one now; you've waited long enough. And you need to let your partner know that it's time for you two to become three (or more).

So the next time you hug him tell him of your plan by whispering it with love in his ear. If he acts as though he hasn't heard what you said, you can whisper again with feeling. And if he gets a little weak in the knees, you're right there to support him. You could start tonight. You could start right now. But you need to start real soon.

The Full Support Hug
(a.k.a., The More to Love Hug)

Recommended Usage: When you may not be in perfect shape, but you're perfect enough for him.

He said he'd support you through thick and thin, but what kind of support does he have on his mind? The moment he grabs you tight by the waist, you start to understand.

He holds you so snug you can barely breathe—you drop from size eight to size six. But the strength of his love feels so great right now, you're happy to take the inches off if he promises to keep his strong hands on." I can't believe it's a girdle!" you tell him, "and I can't believe it isn't!" "But I can believe it's you," you add, as your feet start to leave the ground.

You used to think about joining a gym. Or getting a bike. Or going to a spa. You looked at fad diets, and you thought about fasting. You even considered a personal trainer. But now you know what you really need to get yourself into an hourglass shape. You don't need anything but the man you love, and a personal connection with his powerful hands.

The "It's a Boy!" Hug

Recommended Usage: When you've just received the incredible news that your little star is born.

In the blink of an eye, your life has been transformed. Your hall-of-famer has arrived…call Cooperstown! The future president of the United States is here…alert the Oval Office! And the most amazing thing of all: he's the spitting image of you! Sure, he's only eight pounds, three ounces, but we all have to start somewhere!

When you feel this much pride and joy, you have no reason to keep it inside. So grab whoever is closest and hug them for all your worth. It doesn't matter if it's the doctor, the nurse, your mother-in-law, or someone you don't even know. At times like this, there's no such thing as "a stranger." Hug everybody. Hug them twice. Lift them off the ground, set them back down, and give them a cigar for the road.

Then tiptoe into the recovery room and hold your wife's hand as she rests. You may have just had the longest day of your life, but her day has been much much longer and harder. If there is truly one hero to be recognized right now, the woman you love is that hero. She has always been everything in the world to you, and now she is also the mother of your son.

The "It's a Girl!" Hug

Recommended Usage: When you've just delivered the gift of life, and it is the happiest day of your life.

All the books could not have prepared you. All of the classes could not have prepared you. Being a mother transcends books and classes, and you feel more like a woman than you could ever remember.

As you hold your daughter in your protective arms, you cannot take your eyes away from her. So tiny and fragile, yet so feminine and full of life.

You want to hold her so very tight, but you know you must be careful. Can you give her the care she will need and deserve? Your instincts tell you that you can and you will.

You and your husband now need to hug. All three of you need to feel connected. So spend some tender moments feeling like a family, then close your eyes and let yourself rest. Life is truly a blessed thing, and today you have the proof. She may grow up to be "daddy's little girl," but first and foremost she is your daughter, the child you carried to the miracle of birth.

The "It's Quintuplets!" Hug
(a.k.a., The Fertility Drug Hug)

Recommended Usage: When her labor of love turns into one for the record books.

One…two…three…four…five…you can hardly believe your eyes! The miracle of birth, again and again and again and again.

Right now your wife needs to rest. But she also needs you, and she needs you more than ever. How can you tell her? How can you share the joy you are feeling, and the love that fills your heart? Tomorrow you can buy lots of Huggies, but right now she needs lots of hugs.

So give her five hugs this very instant. Those five hugs will let her know. Five hugs that say you love her. Five hugs that say you always will. Five hugs that say, "We did it together, and did it and did it and did it and did it." Five hugs that say, "Forever."

The "How Did I Ever Make It Without You?" Hug

Recommended Usage: When sunshine comes suddenly into your life and you are overcome by the change in the weather.

Sometimes we forget what a cold, cruel world it is until we find real lasting warmth. Looking back, it's hard to believe you made it on your own this far. But you don't have to look back, because you have so much to look forward to now that you have found someone who really cares.

You have found a partner who makes your life worth living. Someone who accepts you just the way you are. Her calm, loving presence has blown away the clouds. Knowing she's there brightens your world. And just thinking about her for a moment makes you smile the biggest smile. So give her a hug that lets her know how you feel—a hug that speaks volumes, as well as sonnets of love. Pour your heart out as you hold her in your arms, letting her know you've found heaven on earth.

The "Our First Home" Hug

Recommended Usage: When your renting days are over, and your nesting days are about to begin.

You watch the last box come off the truck. The movers collect their fee. After a lifetime of shared walls, basement laundry, no hot water, and nosy neighbors, you've made the great leap. You finally own your first piece of terra firma, and the cozy abode that surrounds you.

If there was ever a cause for quiet celebration, this is it. Whether you do it in your new kitchen, in the spacious yard, in front of that gorgeous woodburning fireplace, or in the middle of an empty room that will someday hold a beautiful crib (or maybe more than one), the two of you need to mark this moment of passage. So get close, get very personal, and give each other a welcoming embrace.

You're home now. Home at last. Home together. And you're here because you did it together. You'll make a thousand happy moments in this house, moments that will become wonderful memories. But today is the greatest moment of all, and your special hug will make it a moment you will always remember.

The Self-concious Adolescent Hug
(a.k.a., The Too Cool to Hug Hug)

Recommended Usage: When you're the new kid on the block, and you're trying to make an impression.

There is nothing worse than being fifteen, especially if you're a guy. You're too young to date, too young to drive, and you still have no choice but to live with your parents. When your mother picks you up at school you pray that no one sees you. When your father drives you to the mall you make believe he's a cabby. You can't wait till you grow up and can talk about this in therapy.

If things weren't tough enough for you, here's the real dilemma: every time you say goodbye your parents always want to hug you. They don't seem to care if the world is watching, they don't seem to see you squirm. You're still their precious little boy, and they want you to know they love you.

What do you do? What do you say? You still live under their roof.

Your only choice is to grin and bear it and try to look aloof. Make it quick, and make a face that says, "I'd rather be anywhere but here." Your friends may tease you but they will understand. They have parents of their own, and hugs they too must endure.

The "Work Is Hell" Hug

Recommended usage: Between the hours of 3 A.M. and 6 A.M., when you have no choice but to open your eyes and meet the day (even if the day still isn't ready to meet you).

The piercing tones of your alarm clock shatter the gentle predawn stillness. It's hours earlier than any human being should have to begin the day. But begin you must. In the darkness you look down at the vague form of your partner lying beside you. Before she drifts off back to sleep, you need a moment of humanness in this inhuman work world. You can't just slip out of bed all alone and start the day. You need to make contact. You need to say "Hello," "Goodbye," "'I love you," and "I hate the fact that you have a normal job with normal hours," and you need to say it all in one hug.

A hug like this requires great finesse. It must be loving, it must be gentle, and it must be brief. A soft rub on the back (one or two strokes maximum), a squeeze of the arm, and a kiss on the hair. That's all for now.

The Group Hug

Recommended Usage: When all of the members of the gang are present, but all of the feelings of togetherness are absent.

Some hugs were only meant for two, but this hug was built with more in mind. Whether it's a group of friends, a group of sworn enemies, or a group of coworkers who are a little of both, there are those times when a bit of closeness can make all of the difference in the way you connect.

So don't sit around waiting for the company picnic, or an executive weekend, or a trip to the woods. Gather your group right now in a circle and snuggle in tight for a big group hug. You're a team. You're a family. You're a clan. You're a gang. You're together more hours than you're apart. Stop trying to hide from each other; it's time that you felt that bond. It may look silly and it may feel foolish, with so many bodies in so little space, but if you can get past the obvious awkwardness, you'll each go home with a smile on your face.

The Powder Keg

Recommended Usage: When the chemistry between you can blow you sky high.

You can hear it in his words and feel it in his touch. You can see it in his eyes from the way he looks right through you. He's through playing around. Right now you're playing with dynamite. And if your guess is right, his passion is about to explode.

Well he's not the only one who is close to combustion. It just so happens that you're in the mood for a little Saturday night nitro of your own. And if the explosion blows you clear into Sunday, you didn't really need the day to rest.

So light the fuse. Pull the pin. Go for the plunger and get blown away. It's the H-bomb and the A-bomb rolled into one, without any risk of fallout. And if your explosion leaves nothing left standing, isn't the floor what you had in mind? Isn't that the position you just applied for? If the bomb squad comes, don't answer your door. And if they send in that little robot, send him out with a note: "We're two adults and we know what we're doing. We apologize for all the noise."

WARNING: The surgeon general does not recommend a steady diet of high explosive hugs but admits there's nothing more exciting than an occasional blast.

The "Just Hug Me" Hug

Recommended Usage: When words could only get in the way.

Don't ask me if I've had a bad day, a bad week, a bad year, or a bad life. Don't ask me if I want to talk about it, if I want to cry, or if I want some time alone. Don't ask me if this means I'm no longer angry or if this means we're more than just friends. Don't ask me anything. Just hug me. Hug me now. And hug me for a really long time.

When you need a hug, there's no need to explain. There's no need to apologize. There's no need to be afraid. And there's no need to be ashamed. The only need is a need to be held. And that's all anyone needs to know.

The World's Greatest Hugger Hug
(a.k.a., The Hugmeister)

Recommended Usage: When you've hugged the rest, and you need to hug the best.

Some days, any hug will do. But not today. Today the longing just won't go away. And you need the hug of all hugs to make it all okay.

We all have one friend whose hugs are a cut above the rest—one special friend who was built to give love. When he holds you he feels larger than life. His arms are immense, and his heart is even bigger. His warmth could melt butter, and his generosity knows no bounds. Some guys are good in a pinch; this guy is best in a clinch. Some guys have the Midas touch; this guy has the magic touch. Some guys are a shoulder to lean on; this guy is a shoulder to grab on. He's the "world's greatest hugger"—it should say it on his business card, and you're lucky to have him in your life.

So pick up the phone and send your S.O.S. Now drive to his house and let him do his best. It's his God-given gift, his reason for being, and he's happy to share it with those who need it most.

The "Give Yourself a Hug" Hug

Recommended Usage: When you can't sit and wait for some kindness from strangers.

You've sold your first novel. You've bought your first car. You've made it through another day at the office. Whatever the reason, you feel like celebrating, and that celebration calls for a big warm hug. But what do you do if you're all alone, if there isn't a friendly pair of arms in sight? Turn to the one person who is always there for you—the person who will always be your very best friend—

the person that is you.

Wrap your arms around yourself tight and give yourself the support that only you can. Let yourself know that you've got a great friend. Let yourself know that someone is listening. No one in the world can take better care of the special person that you see every day in the mirror. It's your first and most important job, a job you can't neglect. Don't feel sad that no one is around. Be glad that you have so much to give. And be glad that you have someone special to give it to.

The "Hug Me When It's Over" Hug

Recommended Usage: When you want to save your strength for the stuff that really counts.

Movies put you to sleep. Concerts put you to sleep. Museums put you to sleep. Parties put you to sleep. Let's face it, and let's face it now, you're not exactly the life of the party. Your wife says she can't take you anywhere, but you don't really agree. Because you always feel refreshed after your little naps, filled with desire for her, and ready to take her "everywhere."

So encourage her to fill the social calendar. You promise not to snore. And when she needs to wake you up, a gentle hug will bring you to full attention. She might complain in public that your snoozing is a bore, but she won't complain when she gets you home and closes that front door.

The Fizzler
(a.k.a., the "Wake Me When It's Over" Hug)

Recommended Usage: When you need to let him know that he doesn't light your fuse.

He's taken you to Paris and London and Rome. You wish you'd stayed home and watched "Seinfeld." He tells you everything you've ever wanted to hear. You wish he'd save his words for someone who cares. Bottom line: He's dull, dull, dull. Dull, dull, dull, dull, dull, dull, dull. And all the money and breeding and looks and Arabian ponies can't undo this one painful fact.

That look in his eyes says he's warm for your form, but it's time this guy was put on ice. And the change needs to be permanent. A kiss is out of the question. And a handshake would be cruel. You need a hug to rescue you…a hug that will make things plain.

As you hold him at a distance with little or no enthusiasm, your final message will be clearly transmitted: "I'm appreciative, but I'm not interested." "I'm grateful, but I'm not giving any." Make it quick to make the message stick. Then go home and take your phone off the hook (forever, if you have to).

The Bear Hug Hug
(a.k.a., The Snug as a Bug in a Rug Hug)

Recommended Usage: When your animal instincts are in good company and it's time to drop down to all fours.

Your romantic mountain hideaway turns out to be more rustic than you had planned. You like all the creature comforts, but all you see here are creatures. When you open the door you're immediately surrounded by lions and tigers and bears...oh my! They are rugs, of course, in front of a roaring fire, but they are not the kind of company you usually keep. You're ready to check out and head back to the city, but your beloved has other ideas in mind. She has taken quite quickly to the giant grizzly, and is already lying scantily clad on this huge floor rug.

Now it's your turn to feel like a wild animal as you forget about the city and get back to your roots. Lying beside her on the wild bear skin, surrounded by oceans of soft bare skin, your primitive urges quickly appear. Prey becomes predator, predator becomes prey, and you're about to get what you prayed for.

From dusk till dawn and dawn till dusk, it's flesh to flesh and skin to skin. Long after the fire has finally died out, the creature inside you will still be smoldering.

The "Don't Muss My Rug" Hug
(a.k.a., The Top Down Hug)

Recommended Usage: When what you lack in daring above the brow you more than make up for below the waist.

What could be more embarrassing than to have your hairpiece exposed in public—for your toupee to take a nose dive or back flip in the hands of your lovely new friend? This very special hug will help you escape all intimate encounters with both your dignity and your rug intact. When the woman you adore comes in for the clinch you cannot throw caution to the wind. Wind, after all, is your public enemy #1, a natural disaster as far as hairpieces are concerned. Sure, you want love. But you can't let your hair down. Not until she knows the truth.

And when she starts to run her fingers through your artificial locks, above all, try to keep your head. Don't panic. Picnic! Take her adoring fingers out of your hair, place them in your mouth, and begin to nibble. And continue to feast on these luscious lady fingers until you know that your rug is out of harm's way.

The Superbowl Frenzy Hug
(a.k.a., The Chugalug Hug)

Recommended Usage: When it's first and ten, and they're about to do it again (see also The "No Brainer" Hug).

It's Superbowl Sunday, the high holiday of sports—you're back at your house, with all your best buddies and your wide-screen TV.

So pour down the sodas and chow down the chips. Suck up the brewskis and throw up the dips. Every point is a cause for celebration. So is each play, each pass and interception. Jump up and down and bang on your shoulders; tear at your shirts, like war-weary soldiers. Knock yourself out, like they do on the field; and collapse in a heap on the living room floor. When your wife comes home, she won't ask any questions; she's witnessed this ritual a few times before.

They call this male bonding. But you call it fun. A room full of "grown-ups" really acting their age. What will you do when the big game is over, and life as you know it has lost its reason? Don't despair. Your friends will be back. Just change the channel—it's basketball season.

The Constant Contact Hug
(a.k.a., The Crazy Glue Hug)

Recommended Usage: When you need a little company for a little longer than usual.

How long have the two of you been apart? Maybe it's only been a day or two, but it feels like forever. And tonight, being even inches apart feels too far apart. Tonight, you need to be close and stay close—to stay connected all through the night. So slide in close on your cozy couch or pillowed bed and prepare for an evening of complete togetherness. Let your arms touch, your legs touch, your shoulders touch, your hands touch. Share your warmth, share your presence. And don't break the connection.

Maybe you'll talk all night or maybe you'll read a book. Maybe you'll make love or maybe you'll watch TV. It doesn't matter what you do. All that matters is that you're doing it together. For as long as you can feel your partner close, your anxious spirit will be calmed and assured. You are not alone and you don't need to feel alone. Let that in and rejoice in your good fortune.

43

The Victory Hug

Recommended Usage: When how you play the game is the only thing that counts, regardless of whether you win or lose.

They said that you had no chance to win. They said you were outclassed and outmatched. They said you weren't just out of your league, but out of your minds for wanting to compete. But "they" don't understand why you play.

The other team was bigger and stronger and faster. But you played your hearts out and never gave up. You practiced every day to get to this point, then you took your best shot and refused to quit. And though the final score says that they won, in no way do you feel like a loser. And in no way could you feel any prouder of your teammates, because you know in your heart that you gave it your all.

So gather round for a final hug, a "victory" hug you all have earned. You may have come out on the losing end, but no one deserves this hug more than you. Because it truly doesn't matter if you win or lose, what matters most is how you play. And you played like the champion sportsmen that you are. And that makes you winners, no matter what the score.

The "Illegal Use of Hands" Hug
(a.k.a. The "If They Don't Call It, It Ain't a Penalty" Hug)

Recommended Usage: When the refs ain't lookin', and your passion is cookin'.

Some women would say you're a total animal. But your woman doesn't follow Emily Post. Your woman follows her instincts, her primitive, powerful animal instincts. And she loves it when you do too. She wants it wild and wicked. She wants it untamed. She wants it "no holds barred." And the best news is, she wants it from you.

While other men may hold the object of their affection like some porcelain doll, you need to handle your woman like the full-blooded female that she is. Touch, rub, grab and grope in a blitzkrieg of passion and desire. Go for the gusto and hold it all close. Tear down the goalposts and dance in the endzone!

There's no need for apologies here. No time for regrets. No penalties will be called. You're absolutely, positively, madly in love and a thousand percent out of control. And that's the way this game should always be played.

45

The Takedown Hug
(appropriate headgear recommended)

Recommended Usage: When two world-class lovers meet their match.

Get toes to toes and nose to nose and stare into each other's eyes. Feel the tension. Feel the energy. Feel the desire. Feel the burn. Are you ready? Are you set? Then wrestle!

Arms flail, legs fly and in moments you're on the mat (or the bed, or the floor) locked in a desperate embrace. It's one point for a reversal and three points for a pin, but there are no losers in this love match, with the possible exception of your neighbors below. You've both trained for a lifetime to meet a worthy opponent. You've survived many losses, mismatches, and ties. But tonight you both take home medals—the gold, the silver, and the bronze—because tonight you take home each other.

WARNING: Consult your physician before starting any strenuous exercise program.

The Stealth Hug

Recommended usage: Under the cover of darkness, behind enemy lines, when you just can't live another minute without a hug.

The air is tense with excitement. You must strike soon, before the light of dawn reveals your position, as well as your intentions. You start your approach. Beneath the quilts, beneath the blankets, and between the sheets, your well-rehearsed movements go undetected by radar. Soon, the target (a.k.a., your sweetheart) is within your grasp. Years of training have prepared you for this moment, and now you're just inches away. Suddenly, the target begins to stir. Your presence has been detected. But it's too late to stop you now. There's no time to protest, no chance to flee. A hug is yours for the taking, and nothing can stop you from hugging with deadly force.

So squeeze and squeeze and squeeze and squeeze. Then squeeze a little harder. You've won this battle. And with this kind of hugging firepower, you'll probably win the war.

Attila the Hug

Recommended Usage: When your thirst for conquest cannot be quenched until you've held her tight.

You've slain your last horde, sacked your last village, struck fear in the hearts of all your enemies. That's why they call you the leader of the pack. But it's not Miller time, it's Attila time, and only one hug stands clear.

A world of riches lies at your feet, and there is only one world that you still desire: the world that hides inside her heart. So have her bathed and brought to your tent. Light the lamps and burn scented oils. Ask your minstrels to play soft chords. The fruits of victory are finally yours.

With all the world in your command, there is only one place for this gorgeous prize: safely tucked into your warrior arms. So take hold of her now and show her no mercy; it isn't mercy that she's looking for. When you conquered the world, you conquered her heart. That's what sacking and pillaging is all about. You came, you saw, and now you will be hugged. Ah yes, it is good to be king!

The Huggy Wuggy

Recommended Usage: When your hearts want to speak, and no one else is listening.

When the two of you are apart, you're both tough and strong. You fight the good fight, and you bring home the bacon. You're two grown adults who get their jobs done.

But when you're alone, your working day done, you both feel like toddlers the moment you touch. So hold each other for balance, and let yourselves regress. It's time for you both to get small. Don't be embarrassed, it just means that you're in love. Together and safe, you don't have to be grown up. As you embrace, you can start with some cooing. Then whisper the sweet nothings that pour from your hearts. She says: "Lovey, dovey". He says: "Honey, bunny." She says: "Baby, Waby." He says: "Cutesie, wootsie." She says: "Cookie, Wookie." He says: "Snuggly, wuggly." And on and on it goes. They may be called "sweet nothings," but they are everything to you.

If anyone heard you, they'd swear you were two years old. They'd tell you to grow up. They'd tell you to act your age. But no one is listening. And so what if they are. Because right now you are two lovers together, completely together, without a care because you're with each other.

The "It's Now or Never" Hug
(a.k.a., The Carpe Diem Hug)

Recommended Usage: When he who hesitates will lose.

You've got to have her now. You've got to have her forever. But does she feel the same way about you? She has given you all of the signals, but how do you know for sure? Sometimes there's only one way to find out. You must seize the moment...and then seize her! Tell her that she's beautiful. Tell her that she's dazzling. Tell her that she's irresistible. Tell her that she's precious. Then tell her the rest with your wild embrace .

To love is to risk, to roll the dice, and today you have to gamble. There are times when the only way to get what you want is to put all you've got on the line. This is not a time to hold anything back. It's not a time to fumble or crumble. You need to be clear, you need to be strong, and you need to be as direct as cupid's arrow. So draw back your bow and take your best shot; shoot straight from your open heart. If you don't do it now, the moment may be lost. It's now or never...your love won't wait!

The "You and Me Against the World" Hug

Recommended Usage: When you're feeling weak, but your love is strong.

Life has its challenges, its difficulties, and its problems, and recently, both of you have had more than your share. If you were on your own, you would have given up a long time ago. You would have thrown in the towel, called it quits. But you're not on your own, and you're not alone, and right now this is something you need to feel.

You have a partner. A best friend. A lover. An ally. A buddy. A mate. And together, you make an army of two. So instead of circling the wagons and preparing to surrender, circle around each other and prepare to overcome. Hold on tight, stay really close, and try to find strength in each other's arms. Remind each other how true it is that it's always darkest just before the dawn. Today it's not a victory hug, but it's an important start. And sooner or later victory will be yours if you remember to always let your love lead the way.

The Uunsolved Mystery Hug
(a.k.a., The Lie Detector)

Recommended Usage: When you've got a lot of questions, but he has very few answers.

What has gone wrong with this Mr. Right? What deep, dark secrets must he be hiding? Does he have a wife in another city? Was he abducted by UFOs? Can it be that he just lost your number or, like your friends say, is he just a jerk?

Sometimes mysteries do get solved, and you'll get your answer when you see him again. How do you know if you can trust what he tells you? Give him this special hug.

You hold him tight and you go through his pockets. You look in his wallet for helpful clues. You hook him up to a lie detector. Then you hire a P.I. to check out all his moves.

It's never over until it's over, and this hug will help you through. It's the hug that says, "I'm glad you're back, but you've got a lot of explaining to do."

The Meltdown Hug

Recommended Usage: When you've run out of reasons for keeping him at a distance, and you know you're only cheating yourself.

You've been fighting the feeling for months and months. But your resistance seems to be wearing thin. Maybe it's because he says all the right things. Maybe it's because he does all the right things. Maybe it's because you've run out of excuses. Or maybe it's because you're ready to try.

So tonight when you turn to say goodbye, you let him get closer and give you a hug. And the moment you touch your world starts to shift. The walls come down. Your heart is revived. And you know deep inside what you've known all along: the reasons you've waited are no reasons at all. This is the man you've always wanted, this is the man you've always needed. This is he-man who will change your life, and you're melting like butter in his caring arms.

Later you can tell him that you're sorry you made him wait. Later you can tell him that he's the most wonderful man on earth. Later you can tell him that you're so glad he didn't go. But now you just should hug him close and feel the precious glow.

The Turbo Hug (a.k.a., The Road Warrior)

Recommended Usage: When it's time to leave the competition in the dust.

It begins like any normal hug. But then her engine warms up and she starts to purr, and when you slip it into second she really starts to hum. That's when you decide to floor it and see what this baby is made of. In no time at all her engine is roaring, her tires are squealing, and you're really hugging those curves.

You're built for speed, but you can tell from the look in her eyes that she thinks you've reached your limit. That's when you hit her with your fuel injectors and really lap the field. Now her chassis is shakin' and her drive shaft is quakin'. But there'll be no breakin' or slowin' down. And that's the moment your turbo kicks in and you blow away the field.

So let 'em eat your dust. Soon you're taking the checkered flag, the winner by a mile. You've set a track record that may never be broken and you've won her heart for good.

The Harley Hug
(weather and police permitting)

Recommended Usage: When you're hangin' on the back of his Harley and startin' to feel hog wild.

Ah, the thrill of the open road. The wind is in your hair. The road is beneath your feet. And your arms are around the man you love—your Sir Galahad and Hell's Angel rolled into one—as he's revving up shamelessly right in front of you.

The faster he goes the tighter you squeeze, and the wilder you begin to feel. This is the time to throw caution to the wind. So then hang on tight for the ride of your life. His engine may be purring like a kitten, but soon he'll be growling like a tiger.

Today this "wild one" is yours.

The Wet 'n' Wild Hug
(shower cap not included)

Recommended Usage: When your baby's wet, and you're feeling wild.

You come home after a long day of work and you hear the shower running. After getting the necessary clearance to part the shower curtains and come in for a landing, you're soon face to shining face with the one you love. With birthday suits donned, and not a shred of clothing between you, you both luxuriate in your own private waterfall. Once soaked from tip to toe, it's time to edge closer for the coup de grace. Wrap your arms gently around your partner, then let every inch of your skin make full body contact. Slip, drip, grip and slide, letting the water ease your glide. If it feels sublime, you known you're doing it right. Even the most virtuous souls need a little R & R sometimes, so don't feel too guilty. Cut yourself some slack and hug away till the reservoirs go dry.

    Note: The "Wet 'n' Wild" Hug is also well suited for fountains, swimming pools, and other watery venues. Please observe local ordinances.

The Warm Snuggly Hug

Recommended Usage: When the only way you'll get some sleep is if you're feeling really safe.

Night after night you barely can sleep and by now you're running on empty. One night it's bills. The next night it's work. And yesterday it was things that go bump in the night. If you don't get some rest you're not going to make it, but with all of these pressures, how can you get some relief? Just when you think you can't find the answer, someone who loves you takes you into his arms.

Pressed against his chest like a baby in a warm snuggly, you know what it's like to be tiny again. You feel his heartbeat and you feel his warm breath, and you feel so safe you can finally rest.

Most of your life you've been too embarrassed to let yourself go and feel like a child. But to feel this young in the arms of someone special is to feel like you're in love for the very first time. So close your eyes and sleep like a baby; let him chase away the monsters that have been on your mind. When you wake up, feeling all grown up, you can thank him for being so kind.

The very best part about being a baby is having parents who know your needs. But everyone needs a protector sometimes, even those babies who are bigger than you.

The Anaconda (some constrictions may apply)

Recommended Usage: When he could use a good squeeze, and you're just the one to squeeze him.

DANGER: WILDLIFE AREA!

When the work day is done you need to shed that corporate skin and slide into something less substantial—something smooth and slinky and soft and slippery, in which you can go after your prey. Tonight the hunter becomes the hunted and the element of surprise gives the advantage you require.

Wrap yourself around his sturdy frame and slowly start to squeeze. At first he thinks you're harmless, just a beautiful creature lost in the woods. But watch the expression change on his face as your hold on him gets stronger. And stronger. And stronger still. He's powerless. He's helpless. He's overwhelmed. He's never felt so frightened and he's never felt so alive. He can't escape; he can barely breathe. And he's loving every minute of it.

He begs for mercy. He begs for more. He begs for mouth-to-mouth resuscitation. Is he a man or is he a mouse? You'll find out soon enough when you release your grip and see if he can charm this snake.

The Vampire Hug
(cape and fangs sold separately)

Recommended Usage: When her blood is making you boil, and you feel a bit like Dracula.

The sun has set, your wings are ready to spread, and you've interviewed your victim. She looks so delicious in your arms tonight, you're not sure you can remember your manners. The nape of her neck looks more like a canapé, and her shoulders look good enough to eat. As she snuggles in close and bares more flesh, your teeth begin to grow. And the scent of her perfume feels like a fine wine to drink down with your meal.

Will she resist? Will she be yours forever? The absence of garlic is your very first clue. Are the mirrors covered? Is there no cross in sight? Then it's time to take your first little bite.

If she suddenly panics and pulls out a stake, be sure to protect your aching heart. But if she moans and sighs and swoons in your arms, just continue with your feast. Her flesh is willing and your appetites have been whetted. It's time to sink your teeth in.

The Frankenhug (some assembly required)

Recommended Usage: When you're feeling kind of foolish cause he looks a little ghoulish.
CAUTION: MAD SCIENTIST AT WORK!

His hair is mussed, his eyes are half closed and his pajamas are drooping. He's not exactly ready to pose for *GQ*. And that makes you love him all the more, and want to give him a huge morning squeeze.

So forget about the fact that you're still dolled in curlers, and don't let your night cream make you hold back. Just grab this creation and squeeze him hard. Lay him out on the bed, strap him down, and give him enough juice to wake the dead. Now stand back and watch as he starts to rise. It's alive!!! It's alive!!! It's alive!!! When he first saw you this morning, you might have reminded him of his Mummy. But once you start grabbing his special parts, he'll know he's in bed with the Shewolf. But always remember you have nothing to fear. Even King Kong could be tamed by a woman's tender touch.

Hugzilla

Recommended Usage: When the monster inside you needs to be tamed.

You will not be stopped. You can not be denied. You crave huge hugs and you must have them NOW! As you comb the streets searching for your object of desire, men, women and children scatter in all directions, fleeing from your path. All fear your wrath. And so they should. All, that is, but one.

When you see her, you must grab her. Then let yourself roar. Tell the universe you have found what you need most. Now tell it again to her.

Holding your precious darling, the raging suddenly stops. There is no need to breathe fire from your mouth. The fire burns inside, white hot and pure. Let it burn eternal. You are not a monster after all. Only a man with an oversized heart.

The Undercover Lover Hug
(a.k.a., The Great Pretender)

Recommended Usage: When the spy who loves you needs a safe haven to hold you until dawn.
WARNING: TOP SECRET; CLASSIFIED MATERIAL.

Above the blankets his presence chills you, but when he goes undercover he knows how to keep you warm. He's your undercover lover, your undercover hugger, your undercover snuggler…the spy who wants in from the cold.

So pull back the bedspread and welcome him in. Give him a safe place to hide. Then cover yourselves so no one can see you and play all night in the dark. He's a master of disguises who is full of wild surprises. He's your very own 007. He leaves you stirred, but never shaken, this man with the master touch. Tell him your secrets. Show him your plans. Tell him the code that opens your heart. Let him shower you with compliments and cover you in jewels. Let nothing come between you but your own soft skin. And if he is gone when the morning breaks, don't let yourself despair. Though the night has a thousand eyes, and to the world he's the great pretender, you are the one secret he would never divulge.

The Driveby Hug

Recommended Usage: When the neighborhood has gone to hell, because the guy you like won't leave you alone.

He told you that the streets where you live weren't safe, but he didn't tell you that he was the reason. Every time he sees you he wants to grab you, and he drives past your house day and night just waiting for a chance to get you close. He's your driveby lover, your driveby hugger, the man who wants to make your dreams come true. And every time you hear his car coming, you know that it's coming just for you. So meet him by the car and give him what he wants as long as he keeps his motor running. If he tries to get fresh you can call the cops, or have his vehicle towed. Some day in the future you'll invite him in, or you'll get in that car and drive off together. But for now all he gets is a quick public squeeze, and this bit of street hugging will have to hold him.

The Overnight Express Hug

Recommended Usage: When you absolutely, positively, have to see her the next business day.

Your hard-working partner is out of town on business, and although she's only been gone a few hours you miss her like crazy already. It's bad enough that both of you will be spending the night apart, and sleeping alone in beds that are meant to hold two. But the post-parting blues need to end there. By the time she wakes up tomorrow morning in a strange new town, you want to be the first person she sees.

So gas up the car, get a good map, and fill your thermos with coffee. If you drive all night you'll be there before dawn, ready to escort her to her first business meeting.

Knock gently on the door so you don't alarm her. And when she calls out that she didn't order room service, tell her that this service is on the house. She'll swing the door wide when she recognizes your voice, and that's the moment you two become one. So close all the curtains, take off your shoes, and hang out the sign that says "Do Not Disturb."

64

The Frequent Flier

Recommended Usage: When her love makes you feel like you're on top of the world, and you want to make it official.

It's day one of your romantic vacation, and soon your plane is airborne. As soon as the aircraft is cruising and stable, lift up the armrest that breaks your connection. Now unfasten your seatbelt, raise your tray table, and get ready for a little turbulence of your own design. If holding her close takes your breath away, remember that there's oxygen handy.

Your plane may be flying at 40,000 feet, but with your arms around each other the sky's the limit. And those fluffy white clouds that pass by your window only confirm what you're already feeling: you're a lot closer to heaven than you've ever been. When the pilot announces it's time to land, you may want to voice an objection. After a higher-than-high connection like this, you may never want to come back to earth.

The Family Affair Hug

Recommended Usage: When you and me and the baby makes three (or four or five or six...) and everyone needs to get in on the act.

It's one of the joys of marital bliss: having a family you can call your own. But too many times we forget to give thanks for all these fine souls who share your name. We get so caught up in day-to-day life that we take our loving family for granted, and in the blink of an eye everyone has grown up and you're barely a family anymore.

So turn off the computer. Turn off the television. And turn off the video games. Turn off the stove if dinner is cooking and gather your tribe in the family room. Get on your knees to level the hugging field, then get in a circle and make a tight huddle. Let the little ones snuggle, the big ones cuddle, the shy ones giggle, and the babies kitchycoo. Everyone needs to get in on the act because it's an act of love. It's a proven fact, the research is clear: the family that hugs together stays together longer. And even when some members have to leave home, they still come back for hugs.

The Weird Aunt Irma Hug
(a.k.a., The Grin and Bear It Hug)

Recommended Usage: When the family gets together, and you want to head for the hills.

She's your weird Aunt Irma and he's your strange Uncle Sol. They look funny. They talk funny. They eat funny. And they smell a little funny. So why aren't you laughing? Because they scare you, that's why. And because whenever they visit they want a big hug.

Hugging these "relations" is a "near-death" experience, and the only way to get through it is to hold your breath. So be a good person and close your eyes tight to prepare yourself for this squeeze from hell. Now clench your teeth, pinch your nose, and open your arms for your once-a-year hugs.

Maybe one day these hugs will pay off. Maybe they'll leave you some cash in their will. But for now it is something you just have to do—part of the price of having family, and a small price to pay to keep two people happy.

The Rock and Roll Hootchie Koo Hug
(a.k.a., The Full-Volume Hug)

Recommended Usage: When you want it bad, you want it hard, and you want it loud.

Tonight's the night. You want to rock the house, wake the neighbors, and make love all night long. Why not let a little bit of nostalgia get you started…a little bit of good old-fashioned rock and roll.

So crank up the stereo and get out those old 45s. Now hold on to your hat, and then hold on to that wild partner of yours. Shake it! Rattle it! Roll around the floor! Goodness! Gracious! Great Balls of Fire! The '60s are back with a vengeance! Elvis lives! And there's a whole lot of shakin' goin' on!

A Minute Waltz just won't do tonight, with its tame sixty seconds of contact. You need hours of bumping and grinding—hours of frantic hugging. And the only way to get it is to rock around the clock!

The Electrifier
(a.k.a., The Circuit Breaker)

Recommended Usage: When your love batteries are low, and your hearts could use a jumpstart.

WARNING: HIGH VOLTAGE AREA! PROCEED WITH CAUTION!

If you need to turn up the juice in your relationship, the first thing you need to do is turn down the lights. So make the room dark, then make your move. Squeeze your loved one tight. Tighter. Tighter still. Feel the current start to flow back and forth between you, like two live wires. Don't break the connection. Turn up the voltage and feel your circuits hum. Is the temperature starting to rise? Is the room starting to glow? Then call the power company and cancel your service. You don't need their help anymore.

Long before Edison used electricity to light up the night, lovers were making sparks fly by connecting soul to soul. So make your connection, make it hot, and make a little history of your own.

The Statue of Liberty Hug
(a.k.a., The Staten Island Special)

Recommended Usage: When seeing America's greatest lady inspires you to hug your own great lady.

It's 2:00 A.M. in the city that never sleeps, and the best part of your date feels like it's just getting started. But where can you go for a few romantic hours if you're tired of all the clubs and the bars? If you've got a warm coat and just a few dollars, the Staten Island Ferry may be your ride. It's a New York institution, it runs all night long, and its decks are filled with couples like you.

As the boat chugs along, away from Manhattan, you and your love are in a world of your own. The stars are out, and you can almost see them through the thick romantic blanket of New York fog. But there is one thing your eyes cannot miss. The great lady of the harbor who welcomes us home…the shining Statue of Liberty. She is what this country is all about: freedom and beauty and peace. Freedom to dream, freedom to speak, freedom to laugh, and freedom to love. And don't forget the freedom to hug, because that is the freedom you need to embrace. So hug your lovely lady as the evening mist surrounds you, and do the Great Lady proud.

The Mount St. Helens Hug

Recommended Usage: When your passion reaches seismic proportions, and your world is about to explode.

Early this morning the first rumblings began when you knew that today was the day you would finally see him. It has been too long. It has felt like forever. And your ground is starting to shake. It started with minor tremors of anticipation, then more insistent shock waves of excitement. You know that when you touch him the earth will move. You just hope you have insurance. When you hear his car you lose your balance. When you see his face, you feel like you're on the fault line. And when he grabs you the room starts to spin. Soon the seismic swinging starts. It's a major volcanic eruption. The lava is flowing. You're off the Richter scale. So hold him tight and ride it out.

The aftershocks will last for weeks. And there will be other repercussions. With this kind of natural chemistry, you may have to move to safer ground. So find a house that can keep you together forever and ever and ever and ever; a house that will stand the test of time because it can survive the mighty temblors that your passion can produce.

The Euro Hug

Recommended Usage: When you wish you could exchange a fistful of American dollars for an armful of hearty European-style hugs.

The Europeans love to hug, and they are not afraid if the whole world sees. Women hug women, men hug men, and no one thinks twice about what that means. Being "continental" means being open to life, and open to the passion that comes from the heart.

So why not pretend that you are living in Europe, up high in the Alps or on the banks of the Seine? Now grab your partner with European feeling and hug with the strength your proud history brings. So many Euros have come to America—why did they leave their warm hugs behind? So many exports arrive at our shores—why is it never the one export we crave? It's time to go back, to cross the big ocean, and fill all our luggage with souvenir hugs.

The Long Goodbye Hug

Recommended Usage: When parting is just too much sweet sorrow, and you need a little something to last you till 'morrow.

That crazy little love bug has bitten you both and the symptoms are already starting. You wish you could be together 24 hours a day. Then you'd never have to say goodbye. But that's not real life. Real life is hard. Sooner or later someone has to go to work. Or go for milk. Even if you were joined at the hip, sooner or later you'd have to separate. How do you survive it? There's only one way: You survive it with the longest loving hug that two human beings can muster.

So don't rush out the door and deny your feelings each time you say goodbye. Instead, spend an extra moment together whenever you have to part. Hug close. Hug tight. Hug until the needle in your heart reads "full." Then hug a little longer to fill your reserves.

You're not saying goodbye forever, only goodbye for now. Being apart won't be easy, it never really is. But being apart will be okay, as your long goodbye hug carries you all the way to your next hello.

The 4th of July Hug

Recommended Usage: When fireworks are in your hearts, and together you are the perfect match.

Every day is the Fourth of July when your heart is filled with passion and promise. So don't sit quietly when you should be making noise. Light up the sky and light up your life. Let the world know how excited you feel. Explosively embrace the one you love.

If you play with fire you could get burned, but if you play with fireworks, the sky's the limit. When you've got nitro in your hearts and TNT in your souls, there's nothing you can do but light the fuse. Like our forefathers who formed a more perfect union, you'll start your union with cannons blazing. Rockets red glare and bombs bursting in air, will give proof through the night that your love is still there.

A rainbow of colors reflect your joy. And the stars in your eyes are a symbol of your commitment. While some use fireworks to declare their independence, your fireworks announce that you surrender to each other.

The Night Before Christmas Hug
(a.k.a., The XXXmas Hug)

Recommended Usage: When your holiday spirits need a little lift and egg nog is not the answer.

> The stockings were hung from the chimney with care,
> Leaving her beautiful shapely thighs bare.
> It's the night before Christmas and all through the house,
> Something is stirring, but it sure ain't no mouse…

When you were young, all you wanted for Christmas was your two front teeth. But you're much older now, and tonight you want someone to sink those teeth into: that gorgeous hunk of woman you call your love.

So turn down the lights and light up that yule log and burn baby burn baby burn baby burn. Grab her beneath the mistletoe and give her a kiss she won't forget. It's your lucky night—you can open one of your presents early. And what a present she is, all wrapped up in sensuous silk and scented with lovely Christmas perfume.

Tug on the bow, watch the knot open, and have a Christmas Eve to remember forever. Santa didn't forget you after all.

The Two Minutes to Midnight Hug (a.k.a., The "Happy New Year" Hug)

Recommended Usage: When the New Year's Eve countdown is about to begin.

When the clocks strike midnight it will be wild in the streets. It will be bodies everywhere, kissing and hugging, jumping up and down and crying with joy. There is, however, only one other body you are interested in tonight. That's why you need to get hold of your partner this very moment and make a connection that will last all year.

So grab each other tight. Clasp your hands behind each other's backs. Now look into each other's eyes and wait for the countdown. 5-4-3-2-1—Pop the Champagne and have a toast. You made it! You're together! Happy New Year!!!

The New Millennium Hug

Recommended Usage: When 2001 isn't just a movie: it will soon be the story of your life.

It's January 1 in the year 2000. The new millennium is here. For some people this will be the scariest day of their lives. But not for you, because you're in love. You have a partner. You have a soul mate. As far as you're concerned, you have it all. And you know that the future is nothing to fear as long as that love keeps growing.

On this very special day you never want to lose sight of the very special person you call your own. Wake together, bathe together, eat together, play together. Set a mood for all your tomorrows by keeping your bond close on this milestone of a day. Most important of all: hug all day.

Tomorrow, there may be times you will have to separate, but there will be no separating today. Today is a day of union and blessing and the first day of the future.

The Soulmate Hug

Recommended usage: When you know each other too well to have ever been strangers in this lifetime.

You've met a lot of wonderful men in your life, but never anyone like this. He seems to see you, understand you, and appreciate you in a way that no one else ever has. You know that you've only just met, yet looking into his eyes, you would swear that you've known him all your life.

You can just imagine the scenario: Two infants, both only hours old, lay side by side in a hospital nursery. One is a little girl, the other, a little boy. They stare into each others eyes for hours and hours. The first friendship, the first bond, the first romance. All too soon, both babies are whisked away in different directions to start their separate lives, and the bond is broken. But then, decades later, an extraordinary twist of fate brings them back together.

Is it possible? It doesn't really matter. What matters is the feeling that you have between you right now. Even if you weren't separated at birth, you still have lots of lost time to make up for. And it all starts with your first hug. This hug requires no preparation, no instruction, no deep thought, and absolutely no effort. So just open your arms and let it happen. Like two halves of the very same puzzle, you're finally coming home.

The Hugged by a Stranger Hug

Recommended Usage: When your heart needs to make a charitable contribution to mankind.

It can happen in a church or synagogue, it can happen at a support group or a Twelve-Step meeting, but it always happens when you least expect it: Someone you do not know, and may never ever know, turns to you in a moment of need, a moment of strength, or a moment of absolute inspiration, and acknowledges your presence with a warm embrace. And for that moment, your spirit transcends. You feel united with all mankind, and with your own loving spirit.

Blessed encounters like this cannot be planned and they cannot be controlled. They cannot be bought and they cannot be sold. But they do happen, and if you keep your heart open, one day they will happen to you.

The Hug in 3D w/Sensurround
(a.k.a., The Blockbuster)

Recommended Usage: When you've got a Hollywood-sized appetite for affection.

More thrills! More chills! More spills! That's hugging in 3D. If you're looking for a connection that's larger than life, hold on tight because you're about to find it. Put on your special 3D specs, take off everything else, and let the games begin. Lights! Camera! Action! It's showtime!

Yikes! Is that a monster on the horizon? No, it's your guy, your very big guy. If you're going to faint, faint right into his arms. Surrender to his strength. Surrender to his power. Surrender to a consuming hug from the beast you call your man. (See also The Schwarzenegger.)

The lights may be out, and the cameras may not be rolling, but the action is going to be nonstop. So make sure there's plenty of popcorn on hand, as you explore new dimdensions of your larger-than-life love.

The Silent Partner Hug

Recommended Usage: When you need action to speak louder than words ever could.

"I know that you love me. You don't need to say it. Tonight you don't need to say a single word. Just come here beside me and put your arms around me as I gently put my arms around you. You are my partner and you are my love. I cannot even think of life without you. The years will go by too quickly for us both, but the one consolation is having each other. You're my silent partner, my reason for living, my very best friend and my greatest joy. You're so much inside me, it's as though you've always been there, and it's hard to ever leave your side. But even if there are times we must part, the trials of life calling us to separate corners, I know in my heart and you know in yours it will never ever be for long. We have taken a vow to always be one, a vow we will honor to the very end. In this beautiful silence, with our beautiful vow, I hold you, my partner, and cherish our bond."

The Book of the Month Hug
(a.k.a., The Best-seller)

Recommended Usage: When you're lost in the stacks and the Dewey Decimal System won't save you.

It's the end of the week and you're pretty exhausted. All you really want to do right now is read a good book. So you go to the library to find something special, not knowing that the one you love is trailing close behind.

At the card catalog he makes his first move, pretending to be someone literary like you. And the moment you start to read *A Tale of Two Cities*, he grabs you by the waist and starts squeezing the Dickens out of you. You want to protest and push him away, but silence is the rule and you're afraid he'll shriek. So when he throws his arms around you, don't throw the book at him. Throw your arms back and drag him into the stacks. This one is going to be a page-turner.

Affection like this has been long overdue, and you don't want to pay the fine. So squeeze your way through facts and fiction, poetry and reference. Squeeze yourselves into the microfiche and read all about the news of your love. Then squeeze yourselves into a conference room and do something wild that's not at all bookish.

The "Fax Me a Hug" Hug
(a.k.a., The All-Business Hug)

Recommended Usage: When business as usual leaves no time for romance.

Have your agent call my manager. Set up a meeting for tomorrow at three. Make sure you have all my beeper numbers. And fax me a photo so I remember your face...

Is this some kind of high-level meeting? Is this how the power brokers play? Or is it just two people who are really busy, and whose romantic relationship only gets in the way. Business is fine when it pays the bills, but you can't be a business machine. If there's no time for love in your job description, then you're going to go bankrupt even if you're in the black. So turn on your fax machine and send your partner a message: I'm coming to see you right now! This message will hold her till you get there in person, to turn your business meeting into a meeting of the hearts.

The "I Can't Wait to Get My Arms Around You" Hug
(a.k.a., The Love Knot)

Recommended Usage: When you need to feel his touch, but it's hours before you can see him.

You watch the office clock as each minute passes. You miss him so much you can't wait for the day to be over. Every thing you see, everything you say, everything you do, reminds you of him. So you stare at his photograph, a picture that's worth a thousand words. But you need more than words right now, you need him there. You want to hold him. You want to squeeze him. You want to feel his loving presence. And you want it all now. Don't despair. Instead, close your eyes and let your imagination run to him. Feel him near you. Feel him touch you. Feel him hold you. Feel him hug you. And bask in all those loving feelings. He may not be with you now, but the feelings are real. And so is the love between you.

Later today, when you are reunited, tell your love about this special day. Tell him about the hug you had together. Did he feel it too? Did he know it was you? Feelings like this transcend time and space, so don't be surprised if his day was brightened. While you were having your fantasy hug, his heart was filled with joy. And for the rest of the day, no matter where he was, all he could think of was you.

The "Don't Bug Me" Hug

Recommended Usage: When you're just not in the mood, and a mood swing is unlikely.

Call it mood, call it hormones, call it being a woman. You don't really care what it's called, it's just the way you feel. How can he feel so different? Can't he read your signals? You'd rather be strolling across hot coals than have him come close to your naked body.

It is precisely for difficult moments like this that this special hug was devised. Instead of having him jump your bones, why not just toss him a bone of your own: a bone-thin hug that will lower his temperature. He needs to get the message that he's not getting the messenger, and your two cold shoulders will make that clear. Give him ten dollars and a list of good movies, then give him a kiss on the cheek. It's your way of telling him as nicely as possible: "Don't go away mad, just go away. You'll thank me later that you did."

The "I Love My Cat" Hug
(a.k.a., The Feline Frenzy)

Recommended Usage: When you just can't resist her feline wiles.

They say that cats are independent. They say that cats are distant and aloof. But "they" must not have any cats. Because you know your cat better than anyone, and you know how much love she really needs.

So the next time your fascinating feline brushes past your leg, scoop her up and hug her tight and fill her heart with love. Smother her with kisses and bury your face in her well-groomed coat. She may squirm and she may writhe and she may protest in song. But she loves this as much as you do, and you're not doing anything wrong.

Some people think that cat lovers must have a soft spot in their heads. But you know that the only soft spot is in your gentle heart, and a warm furry hug hits the spot every time.

The "I Love My Dog" Hug
(a.k.a., The Canine Cuddler)

Recommended Usage: When you just can't resist his canine charms.

He's man's best friend and woman's best friend too. He is loyal, lovable, irresistible, and always there for you. He delights you and surprises you and has a way of being adorable even when he's completely naughty (see also The "Pug" Hug). Admit it. At times you're almost embarrassed by how much you love your dog.

But there's no need to be embarrassed. He's crazy about you too. And sometimes you need to let him know just how mutual that feeling is. So the next time your tail-wagging four-legged friend approaches to say hello, drop down to his level, surround him with your arms, and smother him with love. Rub his ears and scratch his jowls and smooth his shiny coat. Let him lick you from ear to ear as you tell him he's your best friend. Then give him a well-earned bone, and help him bury it in the yard.

The Puppy Love Hug

Recommended Usage: When love has you panting and yipping and yapping and begging for treats from the one you adore.

Just one look into her big brown eyes brought you crashing to your knees. You follow her everywhere like a little dog. You sit up and beg for praise and for crumbs. You'll play fetch for everything her heart desires. And in no time she'll have you housebroken with a litter of your own!

She has you wrapped around her finger, tied to her chain, and that's not a terrible thing. But once in a while you have to show her your pedigree; show her that this helpless little puppy can also be a Great Dane. So give her a squeeze that has some teeth, and don't be afraid to use your canines. Let her know that you're more than just a faithful retriever—you used to run with the wolves. The combination of love and strength is sure to leave her impressed. In no time at all she'll be eating out of your paw, and wild about your new doggy style!

The Bunny Hug

Recommended Usage: Weddings, bar mitzvahs and other large celebrations where the guests are multiplying like rabbits.

It's party time! And you watch in amazement as the long chain of merry people snakes through the room, everyone firmly attached at the hip. Spirits are high and highly consumed. It's a time for all-out celebration—a time for only the best of feelings. It's a time to rejoice and a time to play. And it's time for you to score.

So pick your target carefully. It isn't often that you get a chance to wrap your arms around a complete stranger and completely get away with it (perhaps even get rewarded for it!). Now cut in line and grab on tight. Don't be tentative, don't be shy. It's a party! You're celebrating! You can do anything tonight! Sway with the music and follow the steps. Forward, back, hop, hop, hop. Back, forward, hop, hop, hop. Sure you're embarrassed. Sure it's uncool. But that's also why it's so perfect. And don't forget that no matter how wild it gets, no one will remember in the morning…

The Teddy Bear Hug (no partner required)

Recommended Usage: During thunderstorms, during scary movies, and on cold, lonely nights.

When you were little and you were scared, and Mommy and Daddy were fast asleep in the next room, nothing was more comforting than wrapping your arms around your loving teddy bear. Rocking back and forth, holding Teddy as tight as you could, your fears began to melt. In time, you would slowly drift off to sleep, comforted by the fuzzy warmth of your brown-eyed protector.

You may not be little anymore, but that doesn't mean you don't get scared. And it doesn't mean you don't get lonely. When times are tough, you need to close your eyes and think back to those nights you spent with Teddy. If you still have your Teddy after all these years, you need to find him quickly and hold him really close. But if Teddy is just a memory now, that's okay too. Wrap your arms around yourself as tight as you can, give yourself a loving squeeze, and rock yourself to sleep just like you did when you were small.

The Polar Bear Hug

Recommended Usage: When the weather takes a cold turn, and you start to heat up.

Button up your overcoats and stuff yourselves with down. Lace up your warmest boots, add gloves and scarves and hats. Now dance outdoors in the virgin snow and let your shouts of joy break the eerie silence. Hold hands tight and drop to the ground, making perfect angels. Then grab your fellow angel by the sleeves, hold on tight, and thrash about like wildlife till you're both all covered in thick white coats of snow.

Growl like giant polar bears. Let snowflakes melt on your tongue. And for the absolute coup de grace, let your tongues melt into each other.

Tomorrow the warm sun may come out from behind the clouds to take your winter wonderland away. But today it is yours to make giant snowballs, to romp and stomp and do as you please.

The Panda Bear Hug

Recommended Usage: When you need to share your affections in front of lots of strangers.

With exotic names like Tsing Tsing and Ling Ling, they captured our attention, and captivated huge crowds. Roly, poly, huge, and cuddly, they always seemed to be having such a good time with each other, even when millions of people were watching them play.

Learn a lesson from these exotic imports: take some time to learn how to play. Play with your partner whenever you can, and don't save all your affections for behind closed doors when a bigger playground is waiting outside. Take hold of each other, like two giant pandas, and roll in the yard like it's your wild kingdom. Roll in the park. Roll at the zoo. Keep your clothes on, you don't want to start a riot. You just want to start the kind of hugging momentum you can continue at home.

The gorgeous panda comes from China, where billions of people take pride in this rare treasure from the animal kingdom. Take some pride in your special treasure—couples like you are also quite rare. Take some time from your hectic schedules and go play in public and flaunt your love.

The Grizzly

Recommended Usage: When only you can prevent his forest fire.
WARNING: DO NOT FEED THIS BEAR!

The grizzly hug is too wild for words, and packed with too much action. It's paws and claws everywhere, grabbing and groping, and razor-sharp teeth, gnashing and gnawing. He doesn't want your picnic basket, it's you he wants to picnic on. This is one meal you need to skip. And this fearsone hug is a hug to avoid.

You'll find the wild grizzly at nightclubs and bars, at football games and boxing matches, and at Christmas office parties. If you see one coming, you need to start running. Call animal emergency. Call 911. Call the zoo. Or climb a tree. He may think that he's a honey, but he's really a graceless beast.

The Touch and Go Hug

Recommended Usage: When time is of the essence, but love is the thing that counts.

The phones are ringing. The car outside is honking. The demands of life are driving you mad. Do you race out the door in different directions, barely saying goodbye? Or do you hit the brakes for just a moment, and give some attention to the thing you need most.

Sometimes there is no time to get the hug you need, but just enough time to feel the love you have. Even a touch can say "I love you," and it can say it louder than flowers or cards.

So pause in the doorway and make that moment of contact. Hold each other's hands. Grasp each other's arms. Look in each other's eyes and send the message. It's amazing how far this moment can carry you, making it clear that you're never alone. We go through life settling for less. And sometimes we settle for nothing at all. But love is one place where your needs must be met, even if there are times when they can only be met for a brief and shining moment.

The Hangin' On for Dear Life Hug

Recommended Usage: When life feels like a hurricane, and you've got nothing left to hold on to.

In your world, when it rains, it pours, and it sure is pouring now. It's been challenge after challenge, problem after problem, crisis after crisis, storm after storm, and you've had just about all you can handle. You wish you could rest. You wish you could heal. You wish you could regain some emotional strength. But sometimes there is no rest for the weary, and the writing on the wall tells you the rough times ain't over yet. Can anyone save you? Can anyone help you? Does anyone out there really care? Of course someone cares, and that "someone" is waiting for you to fall into his arms. So run to him now, tell him you need him, and collapse into his powerful embrace. Hold on tight, as tight as you possibly can, until you feel your spirit buoyed by his caring and concern. Don't be afraid and don't be ashamed. Don't apologize for needing his help. Being vulnerable is a beautiful thing to share in the arms of someone you love.

The Hugalicious Hug

Recommended Usage: When you have finally found someone good enough to eat.
Note: No time for this movable feast? Then see The "Hug McMuffin.

She's delicious, she's scrumptious, she's completely mouth-watering. She is absolutely gourmet. This rare delicacy is the woman you love, and a hug from her should be savored. So season her to your special tastes, and let all of your senses in on the act. Start by holding her close to your heart, then bring her slowly close to your mouth. Let your lips caress her, your teeth and tongue nibble her, and your nose inhale her lovely bouquet. She is your "incredible edible." She is five-star dining at its finest. She is better than the rarest caviar and she is ready to be devoured.

Man cannot live by bread alone. But he can live by the hugs of his woman. She is food for the heart, for the head and the soul, and a thrill to be consumed. Wolfgang Puck, eat your heart out, because you have to eat out every night. The finest dining begins at home with a five-course meal of hugalicious hugs.

The Hug McMuffin
(available before 11 A.M., at participating locations)

Recommended Usage: When you don't have time for a breakfast banquet, and a quick love nibble will have to do.

The alarm went off but you slept right through it. Now you've got about fifteen minutes to shower, dress, and get out the door. On mornings like this, you won't have time for a sit-down breakfast full of long, gorgeous hugs. But that doesn't mean you should go to work on an empty stomach. You need a hug that's quick, but that's also warm and tasty. Something that will get you through at least till lunchtime, when you can sneak back home and make up for what you missed. You need the Hug McMuffin.

Pretend you're the muffin and your loved one is the egg. Pressed together, your connection can melt cheese. So give one tight squeeze and then get on your way. Breakfast at Tiffany's it isn't, of course. But it's very fast and that's what you need. So don't be a snob and starve all day just because you can't get a breakfast buffet. Fast food can be food for the soul when it's being served straight from the heart of the one you love.

The Beach Blanket Hug
(a.k.a., The Tide Turner)

Recommended Usage: When the lifeguard isn't looking, and you're hungry like a shark.

At high noon, it was 100 degrees in the bright strong sun. But now the sun is starting to set, and cool breezes off the water are giving you both a chill. Don't get cold, get bold! Grab a corner of your blanket and start to roll. Roll on top of your bathing beauty, grab her with all your might, and keep on rolling with your big beach blanket till you're rolled up nice and tight.

Like two love sausages wrapped in a big warm pancake, all that's missing is the syrup. But this is no breakfast special. It's dinner for two on the warm summer sand, and as much body contact as most states allow. Maybe tonight the sharks aren't biting, but that doesn't mean that you can't start. So nibble, nibble, nibble to your heart's content, but don't get full too quickly. This meal has many courses, and you need to try them all.

The Rainy Day Hug

Recommended Usage: When you could use a little shelter from the storm.

Outside your house it's cold and damp. But today, you don't feel the chill. That's because the one you love is right by your side in your comfy little home for two. So let the raindrops fall all day. Watch them trickle down the window panes and collect in magical puddles. Wrapped in each other's arms, you feel warm and secure. You feel cherished, safe, and blessed. While others are angry and getting drenched, you are feeling no rain.

Maybe you'll go for a romantic walk. Maybe you'll play in those puddles. Or maybe you'll just cuddle and snuggle all day, arms around each other in your cozy bed. It's one of those days when all you need in the world is the company of each other. And lucky you, you've got it right here. Wherever you go you'll be safe and dry as the umbrella called love protects you. So hold on tight and let Mother Nature release her might. Let it rain, let it rain, let it rain…

The Natural Disaster Hug
(a.k.a., The "Hug Me Till It's Over" Hug)

Recommended Usage: When Mother Nature turns into one tough mother.

The best laid plans of mice and men often go astray, because when Mother Nature speaks she has the last word. The howling hurricane outside your door has shaken your life to its foundation. Monsoon, typhoon, tornado, volcano—every natural disaster feels totally disastrous, and the name of the game is survival.

You suddenly realize how fragile life is, and you suddenly realize how precious love is. So hold on tight to the loves of your life—your partner, your pets, your family, your friends—as you huddle and wait out the storm. Those precious antiques that cost all your cash are suddenly up for grabs (the china, the crystal, the paintings, the works). But your most precious possessions, your reasons for living, are right here in your arms. Don't let go of these special treasures. Don't let go until the world feels safe. But squeeze with love and squeeze ever so gently, because there's been more than enough damage already today.

The Lifesaver Hug

Recommended Usage: When the kind of straw that breaks the camel's back just landed on yours.

You've just had a day for the record books. You fought with your mother on the phone. You fought with your sister in person. And you're fighting with your kids every hour on the hour. Your decorator just presented you with a bill that would break the national treasury, your plumber says every pipe in the house needs to be replaced, and your car just died in the driveway. If one more bad thing happens today, there will be nothing left of you but your earrings. And it isn't even noon!

You wish you could go back to bed and start all over again. Or maybe even back to the womb. Then suddenly you look up to see that your night in shining armor has left work early and returned home to rescue you and be at your side.

Don't hold back. Throw your arms around him and let your heart burst with joy. Feel yourself supported and feel your worries and troubles dissolve. His reassuring arms will tell you that you're not alone in this world, and that means everything will be okay. You're not adrift anymore, and you're not going to drown. You have your own personal lifesaver—someone who is devoted to always making your universe a safe and loving place.

The Politically Correct Hug

Recommended Usage: When you need to play it safe, rather than play for keeps.

Note: This hug has been sanitized for no good reason.

When is a hug not a hug? When it is also a political statement. If a hug is "PC," there is no passion and there is no power. There is only appropriateness and politeness and decorum and lots and lots of yawning. No one gets offended. No one gets nervous. No one gets excited. No one gets anything! And that's how you know you're doing it right.

So don't follow your instincts. Follow the book: Approach slowly, exhibit minimal enthusiasm, count to three, then let go and respectfully retreat. That's it. You can breathe again. It's over. You said you were there without saying that you care. No feelings were hurt because no feelings were felt. And that's all you really wanted, wasn't it?

The "As Seen on Oprah" Hug
(for a transcript of this hug, send $5.00 to Oprah Transcripts, TV Land USA)

Recommended Usage: When you want the whole world to know what a great hugger you are.

It started with the DONAHUG—warm, fuzzy, and covered from every camera angle. Then Sally Jessy got wise and her ratings soared. But Oprah is the queen, and when the queen ascended her throne, everyone else moved over or moved on. Hugging became an art form as couples learned to touch, to hold, to cry, and to hawk their tell-all books in front of millions of hungry eyes. When you need to share an intimate moment with ten million strangers, there is no substitute for a made-for-TV hugging moment. You've just been reunited with your lost spouse? Hug! You've just been reunited with your lost twin? Hug! You've just been reunited with your lost multiple personalities? Self-hug! It's your magic moment. The whole world is watching. And millions of VCRs are taping you too.

You've spent hours in makeup getting ready for primetime. Your hair is perfect, and you're miked loud and clear. So give it your best shot and look sincere…and don't forget the obligatory tear.

The "Hold Me" Hug

Recommended Usage: Anytime, anyplace, anywhere, and under any circumstances.

You've got some big news you finally discovered, but don't ask anyone to hold the presses. The news is that *you* are the one who needs holding, and that's the only favor you need to be asking. So go tap a friend, a loved one, a stranger, or even a big old tree. Now hold out your arms and let out your feelings as you release your soul to a genuine hug.

It doesn't matter if you're embarrassed or scared. It doesn't matter if you're lost or in lust. All that matters is that you need to connect, so go make that conneciton now. Let your knees get weak, let your tough facade crumble, and let you eyes get wide as saucers. Hug for hours, even days if you have to, until you have filled up on the thing that you crave. Don't try to fight it, because it's a fight you can't win. When you're hungry, you eat, when you need to be held, you hug. It's just part of life's basic starter kit. Of course there are times when you need to be strong, when you need to be a hero or be in control. But many more times you just need a little contact, and the real hero is the one who gives in.

The "Hide Me" Hug

Recommended Usage: When everyone wants you, but you want out.

What do you do when you can't find time for you? When everyone needs you but you need a break. What do you do when you can't say no, but you're stretching too thin each time you say yes. How do you stop the world for an hour? Or two? Or three? Or the entire day? Where can you hide so that no one can find you? Where can you hide before it's too late?

There is someone who loves you and is ready to hide you, to wrap you in their arms like a big warm coat and shelter you from the cold, tough world. This "someone" is your partner, the love of your life. And this giant embrace is the perfect disguise. Wrapped in these arms, no one can see you. No one can find you. No one can hurt you. No one can ask you for any more favors. No one can ask for the things you can't give.

In just a few minutes you feel yourself grow strong. Being invisible has made you invincible. You're no longer frightened. You don't feel alone. The strength of another has rescued your soul. It feels like great magic, but it's spelled L-O-V-E.

The Died and Gone to Heaven Hug

Recommended Usage: When two souls merge and angels start to sing.

Sometimes, love can feel so perfect that you can't believe its real; and a hug can feel so perfect that you can't believe it's yours. Sometimes, the only way to find what you need most is to lose yourself in your partner's arms. So hold each other close, and let go of everything else in the world. Relax. Release. Drift. Float. When two hearts connect, nothing else really matters. Worries slip away. Fears dissolve. Time stands still. And the promise is yours. Some people wait all their lives to get their little piece of heaven, but you don't have to wait anymore. Your chance has come right here, right now, and all you have to do is let it in. Life doesn't get any better than this. And right now it doesn't have to. You have found your heaven here on earth in the arms of your perfect angel.

The "I'll Never Make It Without a Hug" Hug

Recommended Usage: When you've reached the end of your rope and you desperately need to let go (and fall into someone's arms).

Your mother told you there would be months like this, she just didn't tell you how to survive them. First the job of your dreams disappeared into thin air. Then the house of your dreams disappeared into someone else's possession. And now the man of your dreams is about to disappear into the night, stricken by that disease called commitment-phobia. What is this world coming to? Could anything else go wrong??? If it could, you don't want to know.

Right now you can't think straight. And maybe, you shouldn't be trying to think at all. Maybe all you really need is to feel to feel two strong arms circle around you, giving you comfort and support.

This is no time to be picky; any well-intentioned arms will do. And this is no time to be shy—sometimes you have to ask for what you need. Most of all, this is no time to be strong—it's a time to let someone else be strong for you. So let in that strength, and consolation, and goodwill. Let yourself be hugged for a really long time. All things must pass, including the bad things. Make that passage easier in the arms of someone who cares.

The "I'm In Love with Your Mug" Hug

Recommended usage: When you just can't get enough of that face.

You tell her that she's beautiful and she tells you that you're silly. You tell her that she's absolutely gorgeous and she tells you that her nose is a little crooked, her cheekbones aren't high enough, and her teeth aren't perfect. You tell her that she's the prettiest woman you've ever known and she tells you that you've led a sheltered life. But you don't care what she says. As far as you're concerned, supermodels and starlets pale by comparison. This is the face you want to look at for the rest of your life.

When you think that the woman you love is the most beautiful woman in the world, you need to let her know that over and over and over again. And nothing conveys this sentiment more than a special embrace.

Start by gently taking her head into your hands and staring deeply into her eyes. Stroke her hair softly and slowly draw her closer to you, till your faces almost touch. Let one of your arms drop to her waist so you can hold her tight. Now plant one hundred kisses on her lips, her cheeks, her nose, her eyes, her ears, her chin, her brow, and her hair. Plant one hundred more. Then one hundred more. Then one hundred more… By the thousandth kiss, she's bound to get the message.

The Not Permitted Without a Prescription Hug
(a.k.a., The Under-the-Counter Hug)

Recommended Usage: When you've gotta have it NOW.

You're high as a kite with your feet firmly on the ground. You're feeling no pain, only mountains of pleasure. What's happening to you? Have you lost your mind? No, you've found true love, and every hug from that special someone feels like a little bit more of the drug. But what do you do when you need your "fix" and you're surrounded by a room full of strangers? What do you do when you just can't wait? Here's what you do: You light a fire down below.

You can't get medicine like this over the counter. But you can get it under the table. And that's where you should be right now: under the table, squeezing your baby. So whether you're at your favorite restaurant, at a fabulous party, or at the furniture store of your choice, go below and go for the gold. Above the table things look perfectly civil, but beneath the contact is frantic and fulfilling. No one will notice. And who cares if they do? You're in love. They understand. A hug this good should be against the law. And it probably is illegal in some states. But not in the state you're in right now, that state of bliss that knows no shame.

Note: Do not try to operate any heavy machinery while under the influence of this hug.

The "I Can't Believe I Have to Hug You!" Hug

Recommended Usage: When the only full body contact he deserves is with a giant steamroller.

Why is it that your dreaded "ex" keeps showing up at your family affairs? He doesn't like your family. He just wants to make you crazy. And to top it off, he uses these events as an excuse to put the squeeze on you. His hugs may last less than a minute, but they're taking years off your life. Weddings, house parties, even funerals…this guy really has no shame. Well, you need to show him once and for all that two can play this game.

So arch your back, turn the other cheek, and pretend you hardly know him. Now push him off like the dog that he is and grab the first cute guy you see. You're the perfect lady who has moved on with her life, and he's the perfect creep who keeps chasing his ex-wife.

The "I Just Needed an Excuse for a Hug" Hug
(a.k.a., The Desperado)

Recommended Usage: When it take a little subterfuge to get the love you need.

You'd like a hug. But you're afraid to ask. You need a hug. But you're afraid to look needy. You crave a hug. But you're afraid to seem desperate. What do you do? Where can you turn? Sure you could go to church this Sunday, there's always a hug to be found when the sermon ends. But why wait till Sunday? Life is full of opportunities for a physical connection—places where you can get what you need without giving away your secret—every day of the week, every week of the year. Hang around coat check rooms and help people bundle up. Hang around swimming pools and help people out of the deep end. Hang around photo shoots and help supermodels change their wardrobes. Get the picture? People get the help they need and you get the thing you need most: Contact.

If it feels like a hugless world out there, you're just not using your noggin. There's an endless supply of semi-hugs, demi-hugs, pseudo-hugs, and solid rubs just waiting for you to discover. So what are you waiting for? Get out that front door. Now go and find your share.

The "Love Conquers All" Hug

Recommended Usage: When life puts you to the test, and the only way you're going to pass is in the arms of the one you love.

No one said life would be easy. But lately, anything that can go wrong has gone wrong. The rains have come, your house is leaking, and only your bank account is dry. Even those friends who are always there for you are "otherwise engaged." When the universe tests you, it's no pop quiz.

Sometimes there's nothing you can do but wait until the storm passes. But that doesn't mean you need to be a hero or a martyr. There is one thing that has not been shaken by these strong winds, and that is the bond between you and the one you love. So turn to each other. Nestle and find safe shelter in each other's arms. For this is truly your fortress, the one thing that no storm can shake. And together, your love will triumph.

The "I Can't Help Myself" Hug

Recommended Usage: When holding back any longer could be bad for your health.

He's adorable, sexy, cuddly, and available. The problem is, he's also your boss. You have to see him every day, and that's enough to drive you mad. You wish you could keep things strictly professional, but the only business on your mind is funky monkey business. And you can tell from the way he looks at you that he wants to get into that business too.

But everyone has warned you about office romance, and that always makes you pause. They tell you it's a good way to lose your job, but they never tell you what you could win.

As far as you're concerned right now, both of you are losing. The sexual tension is taking its toll and it's time to try the freeway. So the next time he passes ask him to stop. Then give him a hug that's says you mean business. If he seems confused, tell him you thought it was his birthday. But if he seems relieved, show him who's really the boss.

The Going for the Record Hug

Recommended Usage: When you won't stop hugging until you're in the **Guinness Book of World Records** *(or until the cops break down your door)*

You've waited forever, but now she's yours, and you're so very glad you waited. She's so sensitive, so smart and so lovely: so perfect in every way. But the one thing you never imagined was just how perfect she'd feel in your arms. Holding her has gone to the top of the charts as your favorite thing in the world to do. You'd hug her over a trip to Paris, a trip to Rome, or London. And you'd hug her over a trip to Nirvana, because you're already halfway there.

When something feels this good, why let go? And that's exactly the point of this hug. You did your waiting. It's time to do your hugging. And you're not letting go till the cows come home. You want to hug until your lease runs out, until the planets collide. You want to hug her till the end of time, and you've got a lifetime subscription! The Rockies may crumble and Gibraltar may tumble because they're only made of clay, but this hug is made of stronger stuff, and it's a hug that's here to stay. So open the record books. You've got a new entry. Huggers of the world unite!

The Embraced by the Light Hug

Recommended Usage: When a heavenly feeling makes you light as a feather and your spirit starts to float.

You've read about it in all kinds of books, and heard about it all of your life. You've dreamed about it almost every night, but you never really thought it would happen to you. And you couldn't have imagined it would feel like this. It's the overwhelming feelings of peace, love, and warmth that come from being held in your lover's arms. Did you know each other in a previous life? You feel like you've transcended. You're out of your body, out of your mind, and heading toward nirvana.

If this is a near-death experience, you've never felt more alive. And if this is a near-perfect experience, it's perfect enough for you. Have you been touched by an angel? Embraced by the light? Have you found eternal bliss? Whatever it is that is embracing you now, it certainly feels divine. So embrace it back and let him feel that if he's going to heaven, you're going too. Then let him lift you off the ground and have your out-of-body experience right here in his arms.

The "Just One More Hug" Hug

Recommended Usage: When her plane is on the tarmac, it feels like Casablanca, *and you wish you could stop the film.*

The last call for her flight was minutes ago, and everyone else has boarded the plane. Their luggage is stowed, their seat belts are fastened, and their tray tables are in the upright position. But you and your love are still at the gate, holding on for dear life and unable to let go.

It's just an overnighter but it feels like an eternity. Where's an airline strike when you need one? If you had extra cash you'd buy your own ticket and never leave her side. She's your soul mate, your life mate, your reason for living, and you just can't say goodbye.

So make an impression with one final hug, a lasting impression that will stick to her soul. Squeeze her tight till the jet engines fire, a squeeze that will carry both of you through your post-parting depression. She'll make her flight. You don't have to worry. The flight attendants always help couples in love. And tomorrow night when she's back in your arms, you can fly together, heart to heart, to your own special place in the sun.